Denver

Denver

A Downtown America Book

Karen Spies

dP Dillon Press, Inc. Minneapolis, MN 55415

Library of Congress Cataloging-in-Publication Data

Spies, Karen Bornemann.
Denver / by Karen Spies.
(A Downtown America book)
Includes index.
Summary: Describes the past and present, neighborhoods, historic sites, attractions, and festivals of Denver.
ISBN 0-87518-386-7
1. Denver (Colo.)—Juvenile literature. [1. Denver, (Colo.)]
I. Title. II. Series.
F784.D457S66   1988
978.8'83—dc 19   88-20246
                                                      CIP
                                                       AC

Dillon Press, Inc., 242 Portland Avenue South
Minneapolis, Minnesota 55415

Printed in the United States of America
1 2 3 4 5 6 7 8 9 10 97 96 95 94 93 92 91 90 89 88

To Ed, in memory of Olive

Photographic Acknowledgments

Photographs have been reproduced through the courtesy of Colorado Indian Market (Janet M. Esty); Copper Mountain Resort; Denver Metropolitan Convention and Visitors Bureau; The Denver Partnership; The Denver Public Library, Western History Department; Denver Zoo; Greater Denver Chamber of Commerce; Duane Lofton (Aurora, Colorado); and Snowmass Resort Association.

Contents

Fast Facts about Denver

Denver: Capital of Colorado; Mile High City; Queen City of the Plains

Location: Central Colorado, on the South Platte River, 12 miles (19.3 kilometers) east of the Rocky Mountains

Area: City, 114 square miles (295 square kilometers); consolidated metropolitan area, 4,528 square miles (11,727 square kilometers)

Population (1986 estimate*): City, 505,000; consolidated metropolitan area, 1,847,400

Major Population Groups: Whites (mainly from German, English, Irish, Scottish, French, Italian, and Swedish backgrounds), Hispanics, blacks

Altitude: 5,280 feet (1,609 meters) above sea level

Climate: Denver has 300 days of sunshine per year, with sunny winter days and cool summer nights. Average temperature is 30°F (-1°C) in January, 73°F (23°C) in July; average annual precipitation, including rain and snow, is 15.5 inches (39.4 centimeters)

Founding Date: 1858, incorporated as a city in 1861

City Flag: The yellow circle symbolizes the sun and the gold in the city's history; the blue field stands for Colorado's brilliant skies; and the white jagged line stands for the mountains and their wealth of silver, as well as Colorado's American Indian heritage. The red field stands for the red earth for which the state got its name, Colorado.

City Seal: The City and County of Denver seal is black and gold and shows an American eagle, a shield with a key, a smokestack, the state capitol, and the sun setting over the mountains. The shield and

*U.S. Bureau of the Census 1988 population estimates available in fall 1989; official 1990 census figures available in 1991-92.

key stand for Denver as the key to the Rocky Mountain region. The smokestack was a Denver landmark, torn down in 1950.

Form of Government: Mayor-council, with strong executive powers reserved for the mayor. The City and County of Denver share the same boundaries and perform both city and county functions.

Important Industries: Retail store sales, banking, tourism and transportation, government services, health care, manufacturing, food processing, rocket engines and military weapons, telephone services and equipment, computers and electronics equipment, tires and rubber, energy, beer brewing, agriculture (cut flowers, sugar beets, landscape plants), cable television

Festivals and Parades

January: National Western Stock Show
March: Saint Patrick's Day Parade
May: Spring Fever; Cinco de Mayo
May or June: Capitol Hill People's Fair
June: Sakura Matursi (Cherry Blossom Festival)
June/July: Colorado Renaissance Festival
July: Colorado Indian Market
September: Festival of Mountain and Plain/A Taste of Colorado
September/October: Oktoberfest in Larimer Square
November/December: Christmas Walk in Larimer Square
December: Christmas in the City/Parade of Lights; Colorado Indian Market

For further information about festivals and parades, see agency listed on page 56.

United States

CANADA

Seattle
Olympia
WASHINGTON
Portland
★ Salem
OREGON

MONTANA
★ Helena

NORTH DAKOTA
★ Bismarck

MINNESOTA
Lake Superior

WISCONSIN
St. Paul
Minneapolis ★

SOUTH DAKOTA
★ Pierre

★ Boise
IDAHO

WYOMING

Great Salt Lake

Salt Lake City ★

NEBRASKA

Madison
Milwaukee

Lake
Michigan

Lake
Huron

MICHIGAN
Lansing ★

Lake Erie

Lake Ontario

NEW HAMPSHIRE
VERMONT
Montpelier
Concord

MAINE
★ Augusta

MASSACHUSETTS
Albany ★
Boston
Providence
RHODE ISLAND
Hartford
CONNECTICUT

Sacramento ★
San Francisco
NEVADA

★ Carson City

UTAH

Cheyenne ★

Denver ★

COLORADO

IOWA
Des Moines ★

Lincoln ★
Omaha

Chicago

ILLINOIS

Springfield
★

INDIANA OHIO
★ Indianapolis

Columbus
●

Cleveland
●

Cincinnati

Pittsburgh
●

PENNSYLVANIA

Harrisburg ★

NEW YORK

Trenton
New York City

Philadelphia

NEW JERSEY

WEST
VIRGINIA

Baltimore

Dover DELAWARE

Annapolis
Washington, D.C.

MARYLAND

CALIFORNIA

Las Vegas
●

ARIZONA

Los Angeles
●

San Diego
●

★ Phoenix

● Tucson

Albuquerque
●

NEW MEXICO

★ Santa Fe

Topeka ★

KANSAS

Kansas City
●

Jefferson City ★

St. Louis

MISSOURI

Louisville ★ Frankfort

KENTUCKY

Charleston

Richmond
●

VIRGINIA

Raleigh
●

NORTH CAROLINA

Charlotte
●

Columbia
★

SOUTH CAROLINA

Tulsa ●

Oklahoma City ★

OKLAHOMA

Memphis
●

Little Rock ★

ARKANSAS

Nashville
★

TENNESSEE

Birmingham
●

Atlanta
●

GEORGIA

Fort Worth ● ● Dallas

El Paso
●

TEXAS

San Antonio
★ Austin
Houston
●

LOUISIANA

★ Jackson

MISSISSIPPI

Baton Rouge ●
● New Orleans

★ Montgomery

ALABAMA

Jacksonville
●

Tallahassee ●

St. Petersburg ●
● Tampa

FLORIDA

● Miami

Pacific
Ocean

Atlantic
Ocean

MEXICO

Rio Grande

Gulf of Mexico

U.S.S.R.

ALASKA

● Anchorage

Juneau ●

CANADA

Honolulu ●

HAWAII

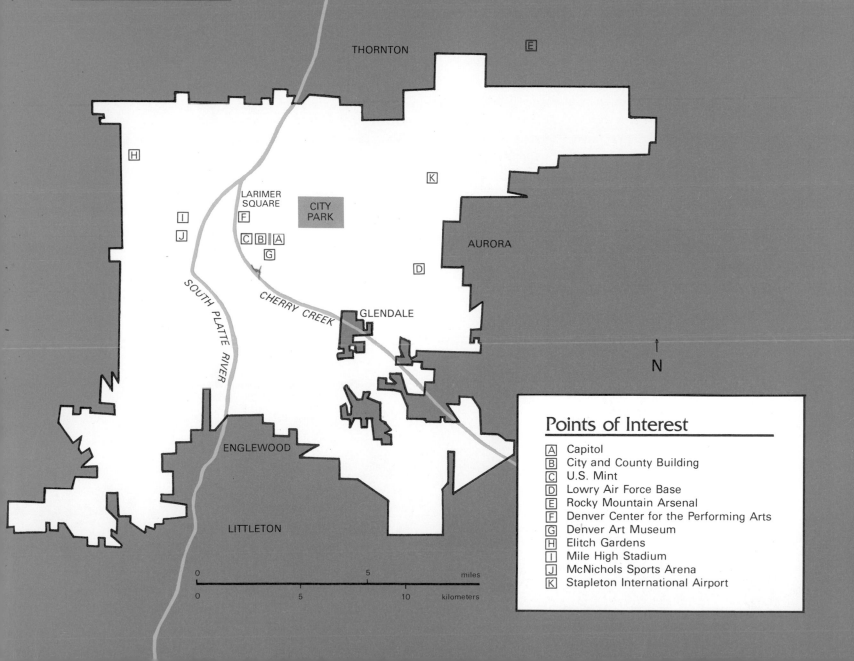

Denver

THORNTON

E

H

LARIMER
SQUARE

CITY
PARK

F

K

I

J

C B A

G

AURORA

D

SOUTH PLATTE RIVER

CHERRY CREEK

GLENDALE

N

ENGLEWOOD

LITTLETON

| 0 | | 5 | | miles |
| 0 | 5 | | 10 | kilometers |

Points of Interest

A Capitol
B City and County Building
C U.S. Mint
D Lowry Air Force Base
E Rocky Mountain Arsenal
F Denver Center for the Performing Arts
G Denver Art Museum
H Elitch Gardens
I Mile High Stadium
J McNichols Sports Arena
K Stapleton International Airport

1

Queen City of the Plains

DENVER INVADED BY SHARKS! Four hundred million years ago, if the city of Denver had existed, that might have been the headline in its newspapers. The area where the city now stands was covered by a huge inland sea. Today, Denver lies 5,280 feet (1,609 meters) above sea level. That's why one of its nicknames is the "Mile High City."

Once a rough Colorado mining town, Denver has since become a modern, bustling city of gleaming skyscrapers and green parks. Denver is also a gateway to some of the world's most majestic scenery—the Rocky Mountains.

The Mile High City is the capital of Colorado. From high atop the golden dome of the capitol building, visitors can see the city's best view of the Rocky Mountains to the west.

Downtown Denver is the commercial center of the Rocky Mountain region. The capitol building is lit up on the left.

Rocky Mountain ski areas are famous for powder snow and sunshine.

The Rockies form a backbone covering about two-fifths of Colorado. To the east are the Great Plains, which stretch north to south through ten states, from the Dakotas to Texas.

Because Denver lies on the flat plains, below the snow-covered mountains, it receives little of the snow that the mountain resorts thrive on. Denver, in fact, gets more sun than either Miami, Florida, or San Diego, California. Each year, the Mile High City enjoys more than three hundred sunny days.

Denver is one of America's fastest-growing cities. About 500,000 people live within the city limits. Nearly two million live in the greater metropolitan area, which includes many suburbs such as Aurora, Thorn-

A ride in a horse-drawn carriage is a relaxing way to see Larimer Square.

ton, Glendale, Littleton, and Englewood. When the city was first planned,
the boundaries were made small. Now
the suburbs have grown and sur-
rounded the city.

Old West history can still be
seen among the city's skyscrapers and
streets. Horse-drawn carriages wind
through Larimer Square, the restored
site of Denver's oldest street. Larimer Street was once home to Bat
Masterson, the gunfighter; Calamity
Jane, the gunslinging cowgirl; William
Henry Jackson, the western photogra-

The Buffalo Bill Memorial Museum on Lookout Mountain.

pher; and "Buffalo Bill" Cody, the famous scout who started a Wild West show.

The Buffalo Bill Memorial Museum and Grave in nearby Golden features silver saddles from Buffalo Bill Cody's Wild West show. In the same area, herds of buffalo are free to roam.

The Great Plains area is still "cattle country," and Denver is the site for the National Western Stock Show and Rodeo. This stock show, the largest in the world, attracts trained

Young visitors to the Western Stock Show discover what it feels like to sit on top of a bull.

The orange and blue clothing of the Broncos' fans stands out at Mile High Stadium.

rodeo performers from many areas to ride bucking broncos and lasso calves. The show also displays the best of the region's cattle.

Even the names of Denver's sports teams reflect the Wild West days. The Broncos play football at Mile High Stadium. The Denver Nuggets play basketball at the McNichols Sports Arena, also the site of the 1988 United States Figure Skating Championships.

Many of Denver's two hundred parks show glimpses of the city's his-

Denverites enjoy the cycling paths in Washington Park.

tory. The city's park system, the largest in the United States, includes the Platte River Greenway System with nearly thirty miles (about forty-eight kilometers) of nature trails. Along the trails lie grassy "pocket parks." In Frontier Park, people come to see Denver's oldest log cabin. The nation's only in-city white-water kayak run flows through Confluence Park, which was one of the area's early settlements.

Ninth Street Historic Park is full of old Victorian cottages. They are now used as college campus offices.

Many other reminders of the Wild West fill Denver. They include the Pioneer Fountain at Colfax Avenue and Broadway and the "Bucking Bronco" statue in Civic Center Park.

Facing this park is Denver's gleaming capitol building, modeled after the one in Washington, D.C. Denver, an important government center, is sometimes called the "second capital of the United States." It has more government offices than any city except Washington, D.C.

When the Capitol was built, the people of Colorado wanted to use materials from the state's own land. They chose gold, representing the gold rush, to cover the dome. The state's miners donated the first coat. A second coat, added in 1950, was very difficult to apply because swarms of gnats kept sticking to it.

Rose onyx, a rare stone found only in Colorado, lines the interior walls of the capitol building. Colorado marble was used for the pillars, even though it would have been cheaper to ship marble from Italy than to bring it down from the Rockies.

Across the park from the Capitol is the City and County Building, which is the headquarters of city and county government. Another famous government office in Denver is the United States Mint, where five billion coins are made yearly. The Mint gives free tours—but no free samples.

Denver also plays an important part in the U.S. government's mil-

The gold dome of the Capitol.

Each December the City and County Building glows with twenty thousand floodlights.

itary and defense programs. Lowry Air Force Base and its Lowry Heritage Museum both lie within the city. Just northeast of the city, Rocky Mountain Arsenal stores military equipment and arms.

In addition to serving as a government center, Denver is the hub of manufacturing and distribution for the Rocky Mountain region. From the coming of the railroad in 1870, Denver has also been a major transportation center linking the East to the West.

Today, Denver attracts people from all over the world. The town that began as a temporary jumping-off place for gold seekers has become a modern city built on its Old West roots. In Denver, it's only a step from a chuck wagon steak house to a symphony concert. The city has earned its nickname as the "Queen City of the Plains."

2

The Boom Town

The carved panels on the brass elevator doors in the capitol building tell the story of Denver's people: how American Indians, miners, and hardy pioneers were later joined by farmers and ranchers. The train panel shows the coming of modern transportation and the people from many countries who came to work on the railroad. The cog wheel panel represents the arrival of workers in modern industry and business. Today, Denver is a mix of all these different kinds of people.

Long before Europeans began to fight over the land, the American Indians roamed the Great Plains. Cheyenne, Arapahoe, and Ute were among the tribes who lived and hunted buffalo on the Colorado plains. Although Denver's native American population is now very small, signs

The brass elevator doors in the Capitol.

An Aztec dancer at the Colorado Indian Market displays his feathered finery.

of their heritage survive in the city. Streets such as Arapahoe Street and Ute Avenue reflect tribal names. In the top of the capitol dome is a stained glass portrait of Ouray, Chief of the Utes, who worked hard to help the new settlers and native Americans get along.

The Denver Art Museum's collection of American Indian artwork is among the world's best. Present-day native American artists from ninety tribes meet twice yearly to display and sell their works at the Colorado Indian Market downtown at Currigan Hall.

Denver also has a rich Hispanic heritage. Today, almost 20 percent of Denver's population is Hispanic, and many city signs are printed in both

Crowds flock to the Cinco de Mayo festival in downtown Denver.

Spanish and English. Colorful Mexican murals brighten the city, and each spring, dancers take part in Cinco de Mayo celebrations honoring an 1862 Mexican army victory over a French force. Denver's first Hispanic mayor, Federico Peña, was elected in 1983.

Spanish influences shaped the city from the beginning. *Colorado* is a Spanish word, meaning "colored red," for the red sandstone found in some parts of the state. During the late seventeenth and early eighteenth centuries, France and Spain both claimed Colorado as their territory.

In 1803, the United States bought eastern and central Colorado from France as part of the Louisiana Purchase. Western Colorado still belonged to Spain until Mexico gained control of the land in 1821. During the Mexican War (1846-1848), the United States won the western region as well.

The settling of the city of Denver itself began about ten years after the Mexican War ended. Gold miners were lured to the area by fantastic tales of great riches. One story told of a man who rolled his wheelbarrow into Cherry Creek and pulled it out covered with gold.

When the gold miners began to stake out their territories, many fights broke out between the new settlers and the native Americans who were already living on the land. In time, the gold seekers started two settlements where the South Platte River meets Cherry Creek. One was called Auraria, which is Latin for "gold." The other was Denver City, named after James W. Denver, the governor of Kansas Territory.

The Denver City group, led by General William Larimer, jumped the land claim of an earlier settlement of miners. Larimer's group squatted on the land for years, trying to win the rights to it. They chose their city name in hopes that Governor Denver would pay them more attention and give them rights to their claim.

This colored lithograph portrays the pioneer settlement of Denver as it looked in 1859.

Gold prospectors used Denver as a jumping-off place to buy supplies for mining.

Few of these miners found any gold, and most of them gave up until a huge strike was discovered near Pikes Peak in 1859. Thousands rushed to Auraria and Denver City to buy supplies, turning the rough settlements into "boom towns."

The next year, the two towns joined together under the name Denver. The early years were tough, because the city suffered fire, floods, drought, and American Indian attacks. Yet the city grew, and Denver became the capital of the new Colorado Territory in 1861. This territory became a state, the Centennial State, one hundred years after the Declaration of Independence was signed in 1776.

In the search for gold, prospectors discovered other riches that helped Denver to become more and more successful: coal, fine clay for making bricks, and vast amounts of silver. With the arrival of the railroad in 1870, Denver's farms, ranches, and businesses were able to send their products all over the United States. The wealth that mining and the railroad brought to Denver continued to make the city thrive.

3

At Home in Denver

Today, Denver reflects the different backgrounds of the people who helped to develop the city. Many blacks first came to Denver to work as railroad porters, dining car cooks, and waiters. To make it easier to get to work, they lived near the rail yards in the Five Points area at the northeast edge of downtown.

The railroad provided transportation for nearby industries, such as the cattle stockyards and the smelters (factories where ore is melted to make pure metal). Many stockyard and smelter workers came from Ireland, Scotland, Italy, Germany, and other European countries. They settled near the rail yards in North Denver, in sections such as Argo and Globeville, which were named after smelters.

North Denver still has many res-

At the Festival of Mountain and Plain/A Taste of Colorado, people from all corners of Denver enjoy the festivities.

Saint Patrick's Day Parade winds through downtown Denver.

taurants, shops, and churches that show the different roots of its residents. Mexican cafés serving tacos and burritos stand near Italian sausage factories and bakeries. Our Lady of Mount Carmel Catholic Church continues to be the religious and social center for Denver's Italian residents. Many Irish railroad workers helped build Saint Patrick's Church in North Denver. Irish pride fills the city during the annual Saint Patrick's Day Parade, which is second in length only to the one in New York City.

Railroad companies also brought many Chinese to Denver in the 1860s. Most settled in what was known as Denver's Chinatown, or "Hop Alley."

The first Japanese who came to

The sharp uniforms of these Saint Patrick's Day Parade marchers reflect their Irish heritage.

The annual Oktoberfest in Larimer Square features music, food, and dancing.

Denver also worked on the railroad. During World War II, many Americans of Japanese ancestry were forced to leave their west coast homes and live in camps in Colorado. The U.S. government feared they would try to help Japan during the war. After the war, they were allowed to leave the camps, and many stayed in Denver.

Today, Sakura Square, with its Tri-State Buddhist Temple, has become a center for Japanese culture. In its specialty stores, buyers can purchase everything from a bokutu (wooden sword) to jars of tofu (bean curd). Tea ceremonies and judo and karate demonstrations are part of the Cherry Blossom Festival, held in Sakura Square. At the Obon Festival, young and old join in joyous Japanese dancing.

Other Asians have settled in Denver, too. Many refugees have come from Laos and Vietnam since 1975. A scattering of Korean churches also reflects the Asian influence.

Hispanics who came to work in the beet fields and mines settled first along the Platte River. Many now live in northern suburbs such as Thornton and close to Our Lady of Guadalupe Church in northwest Denver.

Other parts of Denver show German and Greek influences. In Larimer Square in the fall, polka dancing is part of Oktoberfest, a German celebration patterned after Munich's world-famous harvest festival. The Greek Orthodox Temple in Glendale is the center for celebrations such as the Greek Market Place, where flaky baklava pastry is one of many treats served.

Denver's rich history affects the modern city in many ways. The people from all over the world who helped build the city have shaped Denver into a center of progress and change.

4

All Around the City

Denver's popularity is growing all the time. Millions of people fly in and out of the city from Stapleton International, one of the world's busiest airports. Denver's transportation system has grown from the early railroads to include many interstate highways.

Since most people in the Denver area live outside the city limits, getting to work can be a challenge. Workers used to travel to their jobs on trolleys similar to the bright red Tivoli Trolley, which has been used by downtown shoppers and visitors. Today's workers use the freeways or ride the buses to the downtown area. Smog hangs over the plains of Denver, but Denverites are working to keep their air clean by forming car pools and developing special fuels.

In the city, walking is a popular way to get around. To cross the street,

The free Tivoli Trolley once whisked passengers between the shopping center and downtown Denver.

Sixteenth Street Mall in downtown Denver is designed for people and special shuttle buses.

Denverites use the "Barnes Dance," named after a traffic engineer. At downtown intersections, traffic is stopped in all directions on a red light. People then have the intersection all to themselves and cross in any direction. They even cross diagonally, right through the middle of the intersection.

No cars are allowed on Denver's Sixteenth Street Mall. This street is lined with many shops and features colorful food stands and street musicians.

Although many people come to Denver for fun, the city's booming industries draw many people for jobs. Oil and energy companies have flocked to Denver for years. Colorado's first oil wells were drilled in the 1860s, and today, oil is the state's most important mineral product.

Banking and insurance firms are also important to Denver. The financial district is centered around Seventeenth Street in downtown Denver. Tall, sleek office towers make this business area hard to miss.

While mining gave Denver its start, farming, ranching, and food processing soon became important to the city's growth. Today, livestock and many crops, such as sugar beets and melons, are transported through the Queen City to other parts of the country. Millions of Colorado-grown carnations are also shipped through Denver, the "Carnation Capital of the World."

Most Denverites work in health care and tourist services, stores, or government offices. A favorite government office for visitors is the United States Mint, which contains the second largest gold supply in the country. Most of America's pennies are made in the Mint. Each one is stamped with a tiny "D" below the year to show they were minted in Denver. The Mint has been making coins since 1860, when it was founded by a private banking company. In 1863, the American government bought the minting opera-

tion and outlawed any future private coin-making.

High-technology industries such as computers and communications are beginning to play an important part in Denver's economy. The Denver Technological Center, south of downtown, has brought many such companies to the city. Martin Marietta makes Titan rocket engines for launching satellites.

Denver has schools that provide an education to prepare for any job field. The city has come a long way from the September morning in 1859 when O.J. Goldrick came to town. Dressed in bright yellow gloves and a frock coat, he passed his silk top hat and collected $250 to start Denver's first school.

The Denver public schools, among the finest city school systems in the nation, include the remarkable Emily Griffith Opportunity School. In 1916, Ms. Griffith pioneered the idea of a job training school for dropouts. Today, her school educates thousands of students each year.

The world-famous Outward Bound School trains people to survive and enjoy the wilderness. Workers from many companies also take Outward Bound classes to learn how to work together better.

Denver's colleges and universities include the University of Denver, Regis College, and two seminaries. The downtown Auraria Higher Education Center includes the Community College of Denver, Metropolitan

The United States Mint.

The Denver Center for the Performing Arts includes the Helen Bonfils Theatre Complex.

State College, and the University of Colorado at Denver.

Young people interested in careers in theater or music can study and practice at several places. The Aurora Fox Arts Center and Stage 11 offer acting classes. Musicians can try

out for Denver's Young Artists Orchestra, whose one hundred members perform three concerts a year.

This orchestra is one of many groups that use the huge Denver Center for the Performing Arts. The Center covers four square blocks downtown and offers everything from Broadway shows and modern dance to opera and ballet. In the Center's Boettcher Concert Hall, audiences surround the performers in the world's first concert hall-in-the-round. Among the groups using the Center are the Denver Symphony Orchestra and the Colorado Children's Chorale, which performs in Denver and all over the world.

Denver provides a variety of theaters and other entertainment for the area's many residents. The historic Paramount Theater downtown regularly presents jazz groups, dancers, and children's performers such as Raffi. Children are also entertained by the theater performances at the Arvada Center for the Arts and Humanities and by the Denver Center Theater Company's school touring group.

Denver is a bustling center of activity, filled with hundreds of places to explore. Yet, when Denverites want a rest from city life, the nearby Rocky Mountains offer a welcome change.

5

Denver—Inside and Out

Denverites enjoy their free time. Because of the city's sunny climate, they can play golf and tennis year-round. Even snow doesn't stop Denverites from having fun—they just switch activities to skiing, snowshoeing, or sledding. Their city has more sporting goods stores per person than any other American city.

The Denver park system pioneered the idea of a city owning recreational areas in mountain regions outside its city limits. A circle drive links 20,000 acres (8,100 hectares) of mountain parks. They include the Winter Park Ski Area and the Summit of Mount Evans, which can be reached by driving along the highest road built for automobiles in North America. People come from all over the world for Easter sunrise services at Red Rocks Park. The park features

As a gateway to the Rockies, Denver provides opportunities for all sorts of family fun outdoors.

Many kinds of concerts are given outdoors at the Red Rocks Amphitheater.

a natural amphitheater of red sandstone.

The Rocky Mountains offer downhill and cross-country skiing at more than thirty ski areas. The Winter Park Ski Train is the nation's only train route with service directly to a ski resort. The new sport of snowboarding ("surfing" on the snow) is growing in popularity at many of the ski resorts.

Denver offers many opportunities to learn about nature, since the city is home to a variety of animals.

Prairie dogs dig tunnels in hills located next to shopping centers. Several parks offer fishing. An early morning walk along the Platte River may result in sightings of ducks, geese, muskrats, beavers, or blue herons.

The history of the earth's formation can be explored in Denver at the Rainbow Roadcut, created when Interstate 70 was built. Its brightly colored, slanted stripes of earth contain some of the world's most remarkable fossils.

The Botanic Gardens in Denver display plants such as the Lipstick Plant and the Elephant's Ear. Here, even in winter, papaya and mango trees bear fruit in the indoor conservatory, or greenhouse. Trails wind through thickly planted areas, among goldfish ponds, Japanese gardens, and herb and vegetable gardens.

City Park, a large park just east of downtown Denver, has a golf course, many tennis courts, and a lake with paddleboats. Within its grounds are the world-famous Denver Zoological Gardens. Animals from around the world live at the Denver Zoo, which includes the Children's Zoo and an animal nursery. The Northern Shores exhibit features polar bears and sea lions. Here, a glass-walled tank allows "underwater" viewing. At Summer Safari classes, kids learn how to handle small animals and take "behind-the-scenes" tours of zoo exhibits.

Also on the grounds of City Park is the Denver Museum of Natural His-

tory. A giant gold nugget is displayed in Coors Mineral Hall, and huge dinosaurs tower above visitors. Hands-on classes in the museum's Hall of Life attract curious young people.

The Gates Planetarium is located in the Museum of Natural History. Stars and planets are projected on the large domed ceiling. At the Laserium, colored laser lights flash to the rhythm of music. In the IMAX Theater, adventure and travel films are projected on the huge screen, which is over four stories high and six and one-half stories wide.

Elitch Gardens, a famous amusement park, attracts visitors with roller coasters, a splashy log water ride, and a giant pendulum swing. Lakeside Amusement Park has forty different

Lakeside Amusement Park features fast-moving roller coasters, remote-controlled miniature motorboats, and many rides and games.

At the Denver Zoo, visitors of all ages enjoy watching the animals.

rides and a stock car speedway. At Water World, people can bodysurf on crashing waves in a giant pool.

Many visitors to Denver enjoy learning about the city's early days by visiting the city's historical buildings. Denver's most unusual home was built by a German named Baron Walter von Richthofen. An uncle of Germany's famous Red Baron, he built his castle in Montclair, a suburb which he planned.

The Brown Palace Hotel, built by real estate developer Henry C. Brown in 1892, has a nine-story atrium and a Tiffany glass dome. One of the first "fireproof" American buildings, the "Brown" was the campaign headquarters of President Dwight D. Eisenhower.

The Molly Brown House Museum honors Molly Brown, one of Denver's early and most colorful citizens. She gained fame by rescuing many people when the *Titanic*, a large ocean liner, sank in 1912.

Denver is full of museums, and one of them is designed just for young people—the Children's Museum. One popular section is the Ballroom, where kids can dive and roll around among 80,000 softball-sized plastic balls. In another area, a small supermarket offers life-sized play food samples and a checkout area with a real price scanner.

Four Mile Historic Park is one of Denver's "living history museums." A former stage stop before the last 4-mile (6.4-kilometer) stretch to Den-

The Molly Brown House Museum is one of Denver's many historic preservation projects.

At the Hiwan Homestead Museum, students learn about pioneering skills and crafts.

ver, it now shows what a pioneer village was like. At the Littleton Historical Museum, people work with iron at the blacksmith shop, while farm animals roam the grounds.

Each summer, mountain men gather by the large log cabin of the Hiwan Homestead Museum. In the cabin's rooms, children learn to spin wool, dip candles, and bake journey cake, a dessert made by wagon train pioneers.

The collections of the Museum of Western Art and the Colorado

State History Museum tell the story of tough pioneers, cowboys, and American Indians. More than one-third of all the cowboys were black, and the Black American West Museum and Heritage Center has the best photo collection of black cowboys and pioneers in the West.

Denver has many other museums worth visiting. The Forney Transportation Museum features "Big Boy," one of the largest steam locomotives in the world.

Denver is a city that offers many ways to have fun and many areas to explore. Though proud of its western roots, the city is preparing for the future with its modern businesses and buildings. Now famous for its wonderful climate, its proud citizens, and its great location, Denver is a mile high—and aiming higher.

Places to Visit in Denver

Arvada Center for the Arts and Humanities
6901 Wadsworth Boulevard, Arvada
(303) 422-8050, 431-3080

Black American West Museum
608 26th Street (at Welton Street)
(303) 295-1026

Brown Palace Hotel
321 17th Street (at Tremont Place)
(303) 297-3111

Buffalo Bill Memorial Museum and Grave
Lookout Mountain Park
West on I-70 (exit 256)
(303) 526-0747

Children's Museum
2121 Crescent Drive (exit 211 off I-25)
(303) 433-7433

City and County Building
1437 Bannock Street
(303) 575-2613

City Park
Between 17th and 23rd avenues and York
Street and Colorado Boulevard
(303) 331-4116

Civic Center Park
3-block area bounded by Colfax Avenue,
Cherokee Street, 14th Avenue, and Broadway

Colorado State History Museum
13th and Broadway (next to Civic Center)
(303) 866-3682

Denver Art Museum
100 West 14th Street (just West of Civic
Center)
(303) 575-2793

Denver Botanic Gardens
909 York Street (between Cheesman and
Congress parks)
(303) 331-4000

Denver Center for the Performing Arts
Covers 4 blocks at Champa and 14th
streets
(303) 893-4000

Denver Museum of Natural History
In City Park at the intersection of Colorado
and Montview boulevards
(303) 322-7009

Denver Zoological Gardens (Denver Zoo)
In City Park at East 23rd Avenue and Steele
Street
(303) 331-4110

Elitch Gardens
West 38th Avenue at Tennyson Street
(303) 455-4771

Forney Transportation Museum
1416 Platte Street (Valley Highway at Speer
Boulevard)
(303) 433-3643

Four Mile House Historic Park
715 South Forest Street (at Exposition
Avenue)
(303) 399-1859

Gates Planetarium and Laserium
Parts of the Museum of Natural History (in
City Park at the intersection of Colorado
and Montview boulevards)
(303) 370-6351

Hiwan Homestead Museum
4208 Timbervale Drive, Evergreen (exit
252 off I-70)
(303) 674-6262, 674-5934

IMAX Theater
Part of the Museum of Natural History (in
City Park)
(303) 370-6300

Lakeside Amusement Park
West 44th Avenue and Sheridan Boulevard
(303) 477-1621

Larimer Square
1400 block of Larimer Street
(303) 534-2367

Littleton Historical Museum
6028 South Gallup, Littleton
(303) 795-3850

Lowry Air Force Base/Museum
Enter at security gate at 6th Avenue and
Dayton Street; museum is in Building 880
(303) 370-3028

McNichols Sports Arena
1635 Clay (at 16th Street)
(303) 572-4700

Mile High Stadium
17th and Bryant streets
(303) 458-4850

Molly Brown House Museum
1340 Pennsylvania (2 blocks east of State Capitol)
(303) 832-1421

Museum of Western Art
1727 Tremont Place (between 17th and 18th streets)
(303) 296-1880

Ninth Street Historic Park
Within the Auraria Higher Education Center at 9th and Lawrence streets (Park in Lot G)
(303) 556-8533

Paramount Theater
1621 Glenarm Place (between 16th and 17th streets)
(303) 534-8336, 825-4904

Sakura Square
19th and Lawrence streets
(303) 295-0304

Sixteenth Street Mall
Between Lawrence and Larimer streets
(303) 534-2141

State Capitol
Between East 14th and East Colfax avenues, facing Broadway
(303) 866-2604

Tivoli Denver
9th and Larimer streets
(303) 629-8712

United States Mint
300 block of West Colfax Avenue
(303) 844-3582

Water World
1850 West 89th Avenue, Federal Heights
(303) 427-7873

Additional information can be obtained from:

Denver Metro Convention & Visitors Bureau
225 W. Colfax
Denver, CO 80202
(303) 892-1112

Denver: A Historical Time Line

1850-60s Thousands of miners come in search of gold; few settle in Denver City and Auraria; many early disasters; town held together by a few determined individuals

1858 W. Green Russell and his Cherokee wife are the first settlers; Denver is founded

1859 Gold discovered in Gregory Gulch; Denver has thirty-one saloons, but no churches, schools, banks, or hospitals

1860 Auraria and Denver unite; their populations total 4,749

1861 Denver incorporated as a city

1863 Fire destroys downtown business district

1864 Sand Creek Massacre; estimated six hundred Arapahoe and Cheyenne killed

1867 Denver becomes permanent capital of Colorado Territory

1870s Denver thrives; population multiplies seven times in ten years as many settlers arrive; city becomes successful when it links up with railroad network

1876 Denver becomes capital of Colorado, the new state

1880-90s Population grows from just over 35,000 to nearly 135,000 during silver boom

1893 Growth halts when United States drops silver standard as foundation for currency; many mines close

1900-10s Denver becomes a holiday and health spot for asthma and tuberculosis cures

1904-18 Mayor Robert Speer begins many public works projects, such as Civic Center and many parks

1920-30s A time of stability and regrowth; many social service programs started

1929   Stapleton Airport dedicated

1937   Lowry Field (Lowry Air Force Base) dedicated

1940s   World War II brings many new workers to Denver; after the war, citizens settle throughout the metropolitan area; transportation and energy needs increase

1950s   Denver becomes one of America's fastest growing metropolitan areas; growth is related to the energy boom

1960s   Many neighborhood health programs start up as part of the "War on Poverty"; downtown Denver's buildings are restored

1970s   Construction boom brought on by growth of energy companies

1977   Denver Broncos win American Football Conference Championship; "Broncomania" attacks city (repeat attacks in 1986 and 1987)

1980s   Falling energy prices slow the city's growth; Denver seeks new job opportunities in many fields

1988   Denver approves site for a new international airport; work finally starts on plans for a major new convention center

Index